IMAGES
of Aviation

IN DORSET'S SKIES

Bournemouth's Jet Heritage, now sadly no longer in existence, flew this Hawker Hunter Mk4 G-HHUN in the distinctive bright red colours of Neville Duke's world speed record-breaking aircraft.

IMAGES
of Aviation

IN DORSET'S SKIES

Compiled by
Colin Cruddas

TEMPUS

First published 2000
Copyright © Colin Cruddas, 2000

Tempus Publishing Limited
The Mill, Brimscombe Port,
Stroud, Gloucestershire, GL5 2QG

ISBN 0 7524 1734 7

Typesetting and origination by
Tempus Publishing Limited
Printed in Great Britain by
Midway Clark Printing, Wiltshire

Contents

Acknowledgements

For filling in the gaps in my erstwhile understanding of Dorset's aviation history, my sincere thanks go to: Barry Abraham, Ian Andrews, Joe Ashworth, Maureen Atwell, Peter Berry, Dave Blunden, Anne Burningham, Ron Clear, Ron Davies, Tony Dean, Douglas Fisher, Eric Hayward, Betty Hockey, Harry Holmes, Georgina Hunt, John Lewis, Malcolm Lowe, Roger Marsh, Ron McConkie, John Newall, Keith Norris, Colin Pomeroy, A. Prince, Jon Proctor, Richard Riding, Jerry Shaw, Graham Smith, Terry Waddington, Guy Warner and Dai Watkins.

My grateful appreciation is also extended to the following gentlemen whose willingness to share their specialist knowledge went well beyond the normal call of duty: Jeremy Diack, Frank Hayward, Brian Puckett, Andy Renwick, Richard Tazewell and most especially, my long-standing local expert colleagues, Mike Phipp and Andrew Wright.

I am particularly indebted to the following for their kind permission to reproduce archival Material; Gordon Page (Cobham plc); Dr Michael Fopp (RAF Museum); Barry Guess (British Aerospace Heritage Centre); Fred Ballam (GKN Westland Helicopters Ltd); and the Photographic Section of HMS Osprey.

Finally, but certainly not least, deep and heartfelt thanks go to my wife Thelma for so painstakingly undertaking the editing and word processing of my barely decipherable text.

Author's note:
Whilst every effort has been made to credit individuals and organizations that have supplied photographs, may I apologize for any unintentional omissions, errors or oversights.

Selected Bibliography

Ashworth, C. *Action Stations 5, Military Airfields of the South-West*, Patrick Stephens Ltd
Cook, A. *Airfield Focus 21 Warmwell*, GMS Enterprises
Cruddas, C. *Cobham, The Flying Years*, Chalford Publishing Co. Ltd
Cruddas, C. *In Cobhams' Company*, Dovecote Press
Dawson, L. *Wings Over Dorset*, Dorset Publishing Co.
Falconer, J. *Fighter Airfields of World War II*, Ian Allan Ltd
Legg, R. *Dorset's War 1939-45*, The Wincanton Press
Legg, R. *Dorset Aviation Encyclopaedia*, Dorset Publishing Co.
Mason, I. 'The Spitfires of Warmwell', Dorset County Magazine No.71
Mason, I. 'The Yanks at Warmwell', Dorset County Magazine No.112
Murphy, J. *Dorset at War*, Dorset Publishing Co.
Phipp, M. *History of Dorset and New Forest Airfields*, Minster Press
Phipp, M. *A History of Hurn Airport*, Minster Press
Smith, G. *Dorset Airfields in the Second World War*, Countryside Books

Introduction

To the casual observer, Dorset may appear to be a county not closely associated with aviation. Hampshire and Wiltshire, its immediate neighbours, can, after all, boast such illustrious aeronautical establishments as Farnborough and Boscombe Down within their boundaries. Such links provide these counties with instantly recognizable identities with the air but in the pages which follow, I shall show that Hardy's county has indeed made a significant and fascinating contribution to man's progress in the 'third dimension'. Furthermore, operations at Bournemouth's International Airport are expanding at such a rate that Dorset's fine contribution to aviation seems set to continue well into the new millennium.

It became apparent very early in my research that there still exist strong feelings regarding what many saw as the virtual hijacking of certain parts of Hampshire into Dorset in 1974. While mindful of such a sensitive issue, I have nevertheless allowed myself a broad interpretation of the rules and, for this book, included any location which, although now firmly in Dorset, saw part or even all of its flying activity while resident 'next door'. Christchurch is the most obvious example. Bournemouth itself is arguably less controversial as the history of its airport shows that both counties can lay claim to an equal proprietorial interest.

Although tempted to follow other authors who have included the Royal Naval Air Station at Henstridge in their books on Dorset, I note from the county records that the airfield boundary follows the line that separates Somerset from Dorset almost precisely – with the airfield clearly on the Somerset side. As a means of persuasion, one well-meaning contributor suggested its inclusion on the grounds that while taking off in Somerset, one could hardly avoid crashing in Dorset if heading eastwards. A good try I admit but, in my view, pushing the boundaries of literary licence perhaps just a little too far!

With this slim volume, I do not pretend to cover every location in the county that has hosted flying machines. The First World War stations that housed airships at Moreton, Upton and Powerstock, also a coastal patrol at Chickerell, along with Dorset Gliding Club's present home at Gallows Hill, are, I regret, some of the omissions I have had to make.

Captain aboard! A British Airways Boeing 757 awaits its complement of crew and passengers at Bournemouth.

One

Bournemouth International Airport (formerly RAF Hurn)

Today one passes almost imperceptibly from Bournemouth into Christchurch but at the turn of the twentieth century the two boroughs were separated by a few miles of relatively open countryside. Nevertheless, the flying activities in both areas have, like so many other civic features, always been inextricably linked, a point well illustrated by the fact that Bournemouth's pre-war airport was actually located at Christchurch. To confuse the issue even further, the present-day Bournemouth International Airport lies in a different direction but is still, ironically, in the adjacent borough of Christchurch!

The first purpose-built airfield in what is now the Bournemouth/Christchurch conurbation was built at Southbourne for the 1910 International Aviation Meeting. Soon afterwards, aerodromes appeared at Talbot Village and Moordown (later Ensbury Park) for training Royal Flying Corps pilots. In 1929, Bournemouth Corporation considered four possible sites for a municipal airport after electing not to choose the location at Parley suggested by pioneer airman, Sir Alan Cobham. Today's airport, which is on the site recommended by Cobham, has evolved from what was originally RAF Hurn, a wartime base constructed in 1940 to help offset the threat of a German invasion. It was however not until late 1941 that operational flying got under way when a mixed bag of aircraft that formed the RAF's Telecommunications Flying Unit arrived from Christchurch.

In early 1942, British Overseas Airways Corporation (BOAC) began to use Hurn as its long-haul terminal and military use of the aerodrome also increased rapidly over the two-year period preceding D-Day. The RAF undertook paratroop training and glider-towing exercises before making way for the United States Army Air Force which had chosen Hurn as its base (US Airfield No.492) for the build-up of Operation Torch – the Allied Forces' attack on the German army in North Africa.

Military and civil flying continued to co-exist and alongside the arrival of six squadrons of Typhoon fighter-bombers and two squadrons of Mosquito night-fighters to support the D-Day landings, BOAC set up a special development flight to evaluate new types for future airline use. Following the departure of the RAF squadrons to France, Black Widow night-fighters of the US

Ninth Air Force, and Marauder medium bombers of the 397th Bomb Group operated from Hurn until mid-October 1944 when the Ministry of Civil Aviation took over control of the airfield. At this time, Hurn became Britain's only designated international airport and it retained this status until London's Heathrow opened in July 1946. BOAC carried out its maintenance and crew training at Hurn until 1950 when new occupants took over their hangars, firstly Airspeed, then Portsmouth Aviation and Vickers Armstrong (who later undertook construction and final assembly of the Varsity trainer and Viscount airliner). The RAF's Valiant bombers also flew into Hurn for modification programmes by Vickers which became a founding component of the British Aircraft Corporation on 1 July 1960. By this time, Hurn was an established manufacturing centre and BAC 1-11 airliners began to roll off the assembly lines in 1963 along with major subassemblies for other aircraft, most notably the VC-10, Concorde and Strikemaster. In 1978, British Aircraft Corporation was absorbed into British Aerospace which, as part of a programme to consolidate its operations, closed the Hurn facility in 1984.

The early Fifties saw the formation of Airwork Services Fleet Requirements Unit (Hurn) tasked with providing target aircraft for naval gunnery crews both at home and overseas. In 1972, this unit merged with the Air Direction Unit based at Yeovilton and became the Fleet Requirements and Direction Unit (FRADU). This continued under Airwork's control until the early Eighties when the operation was taken over by the newly-formed FR Aviation. Now absorbed into Bombardier Aerospace, Airwork was one of the many Hurn-based companies that have, over the years, repaired, overhauled and maintained a wide variety of civil and military aircraft. Today, FR Aviation is the leading local company engaged in these activities with, amongst its other facilities, two large purpose-built hangars which have housed RAF VC-10s and Nimrods while undergoing recent major conversion and modification programmes. In addition to this, FR Aviation employs a fleet of over twenty Dassault Falcon 20s to provide airborne warfare training for the armed forces in the UK and other countries.

Charter operations from Hurn began in 1947 when Bath Travel operated flights to Switzerland, but perhaps the company's most memorable flight of this kind was the transporting to New York of GI brides in a Constellation aptly named for the occasion 'Clipper Romance of the Skies'.

Domestic schedules were re-introduced in the early fifties and despite ministerial vacillations and U-turns in airport operating policy, numerous airlines have continued to use Hurn for services to countries which now include the USA. The management of what is now formally referred to as Bournemouth International Airport has experienced, like other similar regional facilities, many twists and turns. The post-war control exercised by the Ministry of Civil Aviation continued until 1961 when the government decreed that ownership should pass to the local authority. The airports at Bournemouth and Eastleigh, both at that time located in Hampshire, then passed into private ownership. Eastleigh, which had recently constructed a new hard runway and having a direct rail link to London, secured most of the airlines' business. By 1967, however, Bournemouth Corporation and Dorset County Council had joined forces to purchase the airport for £750,000 – a surprising but far-sighted move considering the fact that the changes that would bring Bournemouth within the revised county boundary were, at that time, nowhere in sight.

New legislation later forced further privatization and Bournemouth International Airport Plc formally came into being in 1987. Yet another change saw National Express take a 999-year lease on the airport for £7.2 million.

Today, in addition to the College of Air Traffic Control and much varied light industry, the major airport users are FR Aviation, Palmair, European Aviation, Airtours, Ryanair and a vintage aircraft operator, Source Classic Jet.

With upwards of 500,000 passengers expected through the airport in the year 2000, Sir Alan Cobham's 1930s prophecy that the site would provide 'a magnificent aerodrome' appears to have been amply fulfilled.

Colourful posters advertised events commemorating the centenary of the founding of Bournemouth.

This plan of the airfield which hosted the 1910 Bournemouth International Aviation Meeting appeared in 'The Motor' of 14 June 1910.

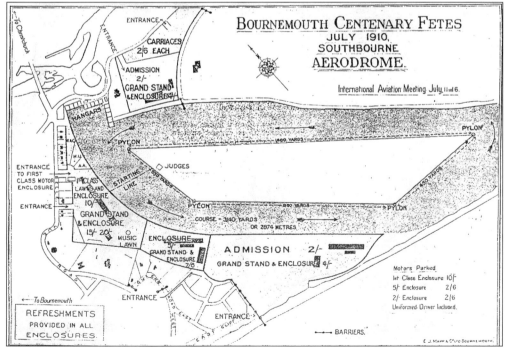

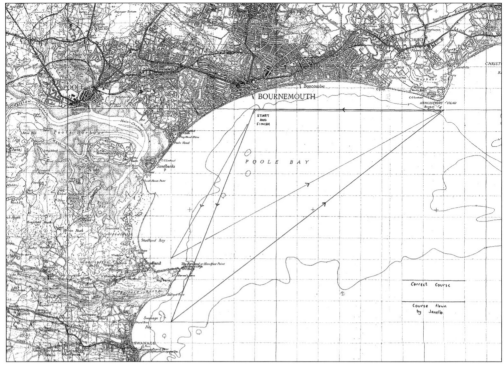

The Schneider Trophy air race was held at Bournemouth in 1919 but dense fog caused every competitor to withdraw except the Italian Guido Janello. Unfortunately, he flew an incorrect course and the race was eventually declared void.

Janello and his Savoia S13.

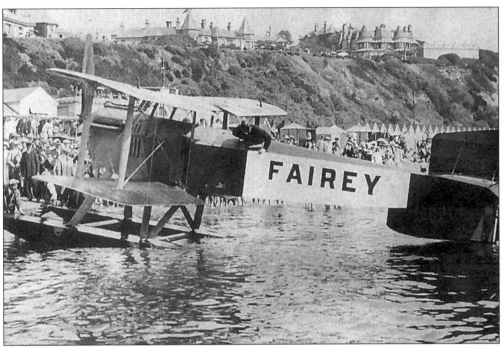

This Fairey III flown in the air race by Vincent Nicholl returned to taxi to the beach. The Russell-Cotes Museum, still a landmark today, can be seen top right.

Bournemouth's race course at Ensbury Park was also used for flying events before separate fatalities brought aviation meets to an end in 1927. Here, Bert Hinkler's Avro Avian chases a de Havilland Moth in that year's Bournemouth Easter Flying Meeting.

Bournemouth's Ensbury Park race course, now long gone, has been overtaken by a modern housing development.

Sir Alan Cobham was a frequent visitor to Ensbury Park and later advised Bournemouth's town council on the best sites for a local airport.

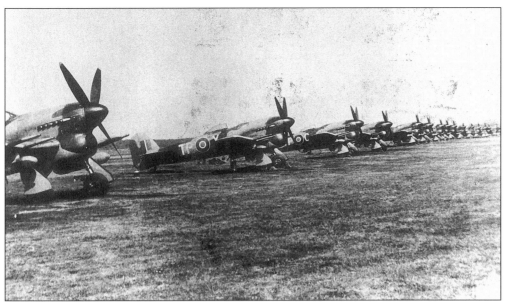

The approach to D-Day saw a massive build-up in aerial strength. Over one hundred Typhoon Ib fighter-bombers (shown here) and some forty Mosquito NF MkXIII night fighters were operating from Hurn in May 1944.

This poor quality but evocative picture shows an aggressively-poised General Eisenhower (centre) with General Montgomery (left) prior to departure from Hurn for Operation Torch in 1942.

A Northrop P-61A Black Widow in the summer of 1944 at Hurn for night-fighter compatibility trials with the RAF's Mosquitos.

B-26 Marauders of the 397th Bomber Group were also based at Hurn for several weeks following D-Day. Crews relax between sorties.

Not all landings were happy ones. B-26 Marauder 'Silver Streak' flown by 1st Lieutenant. L.C. Yeardley comes to rest at the end of Hurn's runway on 26 August 1944. There were no reported casualties on this occasion.

Bournemouth's local entertainment star, Betty Hockey, led a troupe of performers around allied forces' bases in the south prior to D-Day. In order to gain entry to high security areas, she was required to wear a military style (but unofficial) uniform displaying 'Lieutenant's' rank.

Reminiscent of a First World War trench system, this aerial view of RAF Hurn taken on 29 February 1944 shows over one hundred aircraft at dispersal.

This unmarked Wellington is thought to have been engaged on air-to-surface vessel radar trials with the Telecommunications Flying Unit. The ASV Mk III scanner unit is contained in the nose fairing.

On 24 October 1945, an American Overseas Airlines DC-4, 'Flagship London' (similar to the one shown here), carrying thirty-two passengers and ten crew, became the first transatlantic flight to land at Hurn.

The Government belatedly decided that RAF and not BOAC crews would fly Lancastrians from Hurn to Australia in 1945. The aircraft carried nine passengers plus mail.

A BOAC York touches down with at least two engines seemingly out of commission during a crew-training flight.

BOAC's first Argonaut G-ALHC (Packard Merlin-powered DC-4) awaits its paint scheme at Hurn.

A British South American Airways Avro Tudor visits Bournemouth during crew training.

Handley Page Hermes in company with other BOAC aircraft in the north-west corner of the airport.

A typical scene of diversion due to fog at London on 27 November 1948. In the foreground is a Scandinavian Airlines System DC-4 Skymaster.

This QANTAS Constellation is carrying an under-fuselage pannier for additional cargo.

Halifax VIII G-AKEC was entered in the 1950 South Coast Air Race from Hurn to Herne Bay in Kent, by the Lancashire Aircraft Corporation.

Oxfords belonging to BOAC, the Ministry of Civil Aviation and Air Service Training were a common sight at Hurn.

Miles Hawk Trainer Coupe G-AIDF shown in front of the wartime huts (where the present airport terminal now stands).

A Hurn visitor, Hurricane IIC G-AMAU, was frequently raced by the Hawker company during the early 1950s. It is today PZ865 with the RAF's Battle of Britain Flight.

South Coast Air Race competitor Percival Q.6 G-AEYE makes a pretty sight. The photograph was taken on 16 September 1950.

March 1953 and the Vickers team board the 100th Varsity at Hurn before its first flight.

A Viking, Marconi's flying test bed undergoing maintenance at Airwork Ltd. The hangar also appears to be in need of urgent attention!

Another Viking VL 247 of the Queen's Flight ready to roll.

Engine change complete and Marconi's Viking prepares for flight in wintry conditions.

An unusual visitor to Hurn in the mid-1950s was this Lockheed 12A, G-AGTL, owned by Sidney Cotton and used for aerial survey work.

October 1953 – G-AMOO, the first Viscount to be built at Hurn, under construction.

This Mosquito PR16 was one of three ex-Royal Navy machines overhauled for the Israeli Air Force by Independent Air Travel.

This G-ANBO was part of the BOAC Britannia Training Unit based at Hurn between 1956 and 1959.

BOAC also trained its Comet crews at Hurn. Comet I G-ALYS is shown at Bournemouth following diversion from Heathrow on 25 March 1953.

Troops flying out to Cyprus during the Suez crisis in 1956 had to remove their boots before entering this Hurn-based Britannia. The aircraft was about to enter airline service at this stage.

Frequently seen at Hurn in the early 1950s were the Herons of Jersey Airlines.

This Bristol Freighter Mk21 was one of Silver City's cross-Channel fleet. The airline became part of the British United Group on 1 January 1962.

In the early 1950s, Hurn-based Airwork set up a civilian-operated Fleet Requirement Unit (FRU) to provide targets for naval gunnery crews. Shown in this impressive line-up are Seahawks, Sea Fury FB 11s and Meteor TT 20s.

Airwork operated a small number of Firefly TT 4s in its FRU between 1956 and 1958.

Airwork's Meteor TT 20s performed target-towing duties using the turbine-driven ML Aviation winch for deploying and retrieving the target.

The target-towing winch, mounted above the Meteor's starboard wing could not fully haul in and stow the target drogue. This had to be jettisoned over the airfield.

'Cash or credit card, Sir?' – an FRU Meteor TT 20 'tops up'.

Piston power *par excellence*. The Sea Fury's 2,400hp Centaurus dominates this Hurn study.

Airwork's FRU employed Attackers for naval training exercises in the early 1950s but these were replaced by Sea Hawks in 1957. The Sea Hawk (above) sported a distinctive all-over black colour scheme as an aid to visual identification.

Airwork's Sea Hawks gave way in turn to the Scimitar in early 1966. XD 234 is shown here.

The Scimitar proved to be less than ideal for FRU training purposes and was withdrawn in 1970.

G-ASYD, shown here at Hurn in 1967, was a long-serving BAC One-Eleven trials aircraft that was rebuilt as the Series 500 prototype.

A Singapore Air Force Strikemaster in October 1969 in front of Airwork, which at this time handled the type on behalf of BAC.

Between 1968 and 1974, inclusive tour holiday flights to Majorca were organized by Kentways using transports owned by Spantax. Here a Convair CV-990 Coronado leaves its smoky signature over Hurn *en route* to the sun.

British Air Ferries Carvair prepares to depart with cargo for the Channel Islands. It is seen here in 1972.

The Lockspeiser LDA-01 developed by BAC test pilot David Lockspeiser undertook flight trials from the BAC flight shed between 1974 and 1976.

The late seventies saw the setting up of the 'ROMBAC' deal allowing the BAC One-Eleven to be manufactured in Romania. Antonov AN-26s operated by Tarom were frequently used to transport cargo between the manufacturing centres.

Another machine used by Tarom for moving equipment was the Boeing 707C, caught here in wet conditions at Hurn.

Not much doubt where this picture was taken. Dan-Air operated HS 748s on its 'Link City' services to Birmingham, Liverpool/Manchester and Newcastle from 1972 to 1987.

An Air Sarnia Trislander takes on fuel while an Aviogenex Boeing 737 awaits taxiing clearance.

Having resided at Hurn-Bournemouth for thirty-eight years, the Handley Page Herald finally said its farewell when Channel Express withdrew G-BEYF from service in April 1999.

When Flight Refuelling's Airfield Division transferred from Tarrant Rushton to Hurn in 1980, it was engaged in the conversion of three Sea Vixens to the D.Mk3 (pilot-less drone) configuration.

Cancellation of the Sea Vixen drone development programme saw Flight Refuelling and Flight Systems Inc. submit a joint proposal to convert Super Sabres into QF-100 unmanned target aircraft.

No warlike pretensions here. Nigel Reid's beautifully restored DH.60 G Gipsy Moth brings a touch of nostalgia to Bournemouth's Flying Club in September 1996. This aircraft first flew with the club when it was resident at Christchurch airfield in 1936.

Airport life seen from a different angle – an air traffic controller guides a Futura Boeing 737 towards the terminal area.

In the early 1990s, FLS Aerospace marketed the Optica and three new aircraft were built at Bournemouth. Seen here is G-BMPL in 1997.

Goodyear's 'Blimp' was a regular visitor to Bournemouth during summer months in the early 1990s.

Today, following the demise of Jet Heritage, the sole operator of vintage military aircraft such as this DH Venom FB 50, is Bournemouth's Source Classic Jet.

Venoms and Vamps! Seen here on the hard-standing are two of Source Classic's fleet of twin boomers, DH Venom FB 50, WE 275 (foreground) and DH Vampire T.55, WZ 589.

The DC-3 has, in one form or another, been in constant evidence at Bournemouth since wartime days. South Coast Airways still maintains the tradition using G-DAKK for local pleasure flights.

Born out of Flight Refuelling's Airfield Division in 1985, FR Aviation employs a large fleet of Dassault Falcon 20 aircraft to provide electronic warfare training for UK and other armed services.

Until superseded by BAe Hawks, Hunters from RNAS Yeovilton accompanied FR Aviation's Falcons in training ships' weapon system crews to combat aerial attack.

FR Aviation also undertakes the maintenance and modification of the RAF's existing Canberras.

A VC-10 two-point tanker carrying air-to-air refuelling pods on each wing, makes an impressive appearance at a Bournemouth air show.

During the 1990s, FR Aviation constructed two large hangars which now dominate the Bournemouth Airport skyline. These were built to accommodate VC 10s during a major tanker conversion programme and the first four Nimrods, shown here undergoing reconfiguration to MRA 4 standard.

Old friends do pop in from time to time. FR Aviation plays host to Concorde during an overnight stopover in November 1999.

Bournemouth's airport passenger reception area (right) offers a leisurely atmosphere.

'Scene' in context, this picture of the airport in the 1990s provides an interesting contrast to the wartime layout shown on page 18. The old British Aerospace complex is at centre (top), FR Avation centre (right), and the main passenger reception and dispersal area is centre (lower).

Two

Christchurch (Bournemouth) Airport (RAF Christchurch)

The rudimentary airshow performed by Surrey Flying Services at Burry's Farm, Mudeford in 1926 is generally regarded as the day aviation first came to Christchurch. Another famous performer, Sir Alan Cobham, also brought his National Aviation Day team of fliers to Burry's Farm in 1933. Shortly afterwards he was invited by a local pilot, Francis Fisher (Fisher Aviation) and landowners, Albert and Harold Burry to set up a 'proper' aerodrome on the site. Accordingly, a new company called Bournemouth Airport Ltd was opened in April 1935 with Cobham Air Routes, and Portsmouth, Southsea and Isle of Wight Aviation prominent among several airlines operating from the airfield.

A military flavour was introduced when, in 1937, the first of several Empire Air Day Displays took place and in the wake of the Munich crisis the following year, Bournemouth Flying Club, by now resident at the airport, joined the Civil Air Guard scheme in order to train pilots. In 1940, however, this was brought to a halt when the government bought the airfield, stopped unnecessary civil flying and requisitioned all private aircraft. Among the first service arrivals at what had now become RAF Christchurch were three elderly Avro 504s. These were used in trials to determine the radar image of wooden gliders which were towed out almost to the French coast before being released to simulate an enemy airborne attack on the Dorset cliffs near Swanage. Serious military activity at Christchurch, however, began in April 1940 when the RAF's Special Duties Flight (SDF) – a vague designation for aircraft engaged in radar direction finding experiments – flew in a miscellaneous collection of Blenheims, Ansons, Harrows and later, Wellingtons.

On 30 April 1941, a Bucker Jungmann training biplane, stolen from Caen by two French Air Force pilots, landed at Christchurch. As might be expected this daring feat made headlines at the time but the aircraft, displayed in London during 'War Weapons Week' suffered badly at the hands of souvenir hunters and was subsequently scrapped. Also in 1941, the SDF was absorbed into the Telecommunications Flying Unit (TFU) nominally based at nearby Hurn but using Christchurch as a satellite base. Shortly afterwards, the TFU and associated

Telecommunications Research Establishment at Worth Matravers left for Defford and Great Malvern. From 1941, Airspeed Ltd operated a shadow factory adjacent to the aerodrome, producing Oxford trainers, Horsa gliders and, later, Mosquitos.

Life at RAF Christchurch changed dramatically with the arrival of the 405th Fighter Bomber Group in March 1944. The senior officers of what was now also US Station 416 were housed in Bure Homage Manor House, the aircrew in nearby private dwellings and ground crew in pyramid tents on the airfield perimeter. The Group consisted of 509, 510 and 511 Fighter Bomber squadrons which, equipped with Thunderbolts, took part in sweeps over France, and bomber escort duties.

Mention of the American presence at Christchurch cannot pass without due credit being given to the enormous effort of the US 833 Aviation Engineer Battalion which, in just three days, bulldozed a 4,800ft-long runway, covering it with Sommerfeld tracking on bitumenized hessian underlay. Conditions were primitive for the enlisted men and once a week they were taken to the Royal Bath Hotel in Bournemouth for, appropriately enough, a bath!

Following the departure of TFU, the Naval Airborne Radio Installation Unit arrived with a large variety of Fleet Air Arm aircraft. Designated HMS Raven and administered from its parent unit at Eastleigh, its work included the fitting of Airborne Interception radar into Fulmar fighters of the Naval Night Fighter Interception Unit and Air-to-Surface radar into many other types of aircraft. In addition to this wide range of inter-service activity, many Special Operations Executive (SOE) agents who were based in 'The House in the Woods' at Beaulieu, were flown from the airfield in great secrecy in special black-painted Lysanders.

By 1946, all military flying at Christchurch had ceased with the exception of No.622 Gliding School which continued to operate until it moved to Old Sarum in the early 1960s. Following the formal closure of the airfield in 1964, housing development has largely overtaken the site. The only reminders of its worthy past are now road signs bearing the names of once familiar aircraft and an ex-Royal Navy 899 Squadron Sea Vixen that throughout the 1980s and 1990s has been displayed alongside the old Airspeed factory entrance. Sadly, following repeated acts of vandalism, it has recently been decided to move this treasured exhibit to the Tangmere Air Museum.

Prior to the development of Christchurch's airport at what was originally Burry's Farm, aviating also took place at Francis Fisher's flying field at Somerford Bridge. This picture shows fairground-style barkers encouraging a seemingly non-existent crowd to experience the 'thrill of the air' at Somerford Bridge at Whitsuntide, 1933.

BOURNEMOUTH AIRPORT LTD
1935 - 39

Christchurch (Bournemouth) Airport's proximity to the town's harbour and coastline is clearly shown here.

Captain Fisher's Avro 504K, powered by a 110hp Le Rhone rotary engine, was a familiar sight over the Dorset coast in the 1930s.

Francis Fisher's machine *en route* to a servicing assignment at a garage in nearby Tuckton.

In 1940, Avro 504Ns flew from Christchurch to a landing ground near the experimental radar station at Worth Matravers before returning at the end of each day's work

In the mid-1930s, Sir Alan Cobam (right) was concurrently the managing director of Cobham Air Routes (which operated from Christchurch), a director of Airspeeds Ltd (which supplied Envoys and Couriers to Cobham Air Routes), chairman of Portsmouth, Southsea and I.O.W. Aviation (which also operated from Christchurch) and a director of Bournemouth Airport. A vested interest arrangement such as this would certainly cause raised eyebrows at today's Monopolies Commission!

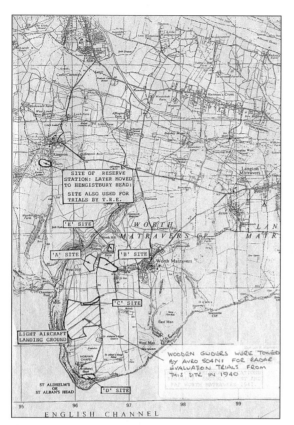

Worth Matravers near Swanage was home to Telecommunications Research Establishment scientists and the site of a Chain Home early warning station at the start of the war.

Personnel from Worth Matravers with Flt Lt. Dunlop of the Special Duties Flight outside the Duty Pilot Hut at Christchurch in 1941.
From left to right: M. Capelli, D. Fisher, N. Holdsworth and Dr F.C. Williams. (Flt Lt. Dunlop was killed on 30 October 1941.)

This scene at Worth Matravers in 1940 shows the bomb blast barriers surrounding the TRE huts and one of the Chain Home transmitting towers.

The Bucker Jungmann trainer hijacked by two French Air Force pilots who, according to a confidential report, flew it to Christchurch and freedom on 30 April 1941. The date recorded on the descriptive board is apparently incorrect. Colonel Valin, C.-in-C. Free French Air Force, stands alongside.

Flight Sgt. Pritchard, a fluent French speaker, escorted the two escapees, Denys Boudard and Jean Herbert, to London for interrogation.

Whitley N1370, still showing 102 Squadron codes, shows its long-range Air-to-Surface Vessel radar aerial arrays to advantage.

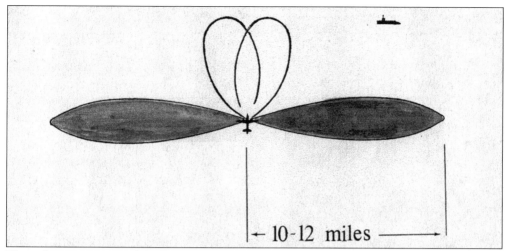

← 10-12 miles ⟶

The radiation pattern of the long-range ASV radar which swept a sea area of roughly twenty miles in width. Used in conjunction with the powerful Leigh searchlight, ASV assisted in the destruction of many U-boats by RAF Coastal Command aircraft.

Airspeed's Christchurch shadow factory is shown at the top left corner of the airfield. The area to the right of the wood (which formed part of the pre-war airfield boundary) was used by the US 405th Fighter Group.

The Airspeed factory adjacent to Somerford Road, with the Isle of Wight visible in the far distance.

A Bedford Armadillo Mk3 armoured three-ton lorry (shown) and two Bedford. Armadillo 30cwt armoured lorries fitted with Hotchkiss machine-guns were used for Christchurch Airfield's defence. A 112-pounder anti-Zeppelin gun and a machine-gun were also positioned at the southern end of the airfield.

The three blister hangars shown here were erected later in the war.

A very unusual type that formed part of the Special Duties Flight was this Boeing 247, DZ 203 fitted with American 10cm Airborne Interception radar.

Boulton Paul Defiants, unsuccessful as fighters in the Battle of Britain, were relegated to target-towing duties at Christchurch.

A variety of aircraft were used by the SDF to evaluate Airborne Interception radar. The 'thimble nose' fairing houses the scanner in this prototype Beaufighter.

This civil-registered DC-3, G-AGGB, which arrived at Christchurch on 8 February 1941, was probably the largest machine to have used the pre-war Bournemouth Airport. The Operations Record Book entry for this date states 'KLM DC 3 arrived for conveyance of an IMPORTANT PERSON TO LISBON.' This was President Roosevelt's special aide, Harry Hopkins. The aircraft was eventually lost on 1 June 1943 returning from Lisbon with thirteen passengers that included film actor Leslie Howard.

Airspeed's main wartime activity centred on the production of Oxford trainers (559 built at Christchurch), Horsa gliders (665) and Mosquitos (122). Horsas await flight test in 1943.

Prior to D-Day, 'Razorback' P-47D Thunderbolts of the US 509, 510 and 511 Fighter Bomber Squadrons based at Christchurch regularly undertook wave attacks, involving some fifty aircraft, on enemy coastal targets. The 405th Fighter Group left for France on 11 July 1944.

In the closing stages of the war, the Naval Air Radio Installation Unit (NARIU) carried out equipment trials on virtually every type of aircraft operated by the Fleet Air Arm. NARIU finally left Christchurch (HMS Raven) in late 1945.

This Avro Anson carrying a LOPGAP (Liquid Oxygen-Petrol Guided Anti-aircraft Projectile) – shown mounted back-to-front for trial purposes – was operated by NARIU. This was the UK's first attempt to build a guided missile.

NAIRU installed Airborne Interception radar into Fairey Fulmar shipborne fighters.

Black-painted Lysanders were used for flying SOE agents from Christchurch to France.

Although taken over by de Havilland in 1930, Airspeed Ltd continued to produce its own designs throughout the war. However, when the two companies finally merged in 1951, Christchurch became the home of Airspeed Division of the de Havilland Co. Ltd. This picture shows the factory decorated for the Queen's Coronation in 1953.

Ron Clear, an Airspeed test pilot from the late 1930s, went on to fly with de Havilland, Hawker Siddeley and British Aerospace. The Sea Vixen shown in this photograph resided for many years outside the old factory site in Somerford Road.

Sweet and Low – a D H Venom NF 3 piloted by Red Armstrong – sweeps in over Christchurch in 1953.

The prototype DH Vampire T 11
trainer midst sunshine and
showers.

Home-grown at Christchurch!
The Needles provide a striking
background for this production
standard DH Sea Vixen.

Let's talk Ambassadors! Prototypes G-ALFR and G-AMAD taxi out at Christchurch.

Superb access to the Centaurus' 'power egg' was the result of clever cowling design.

'Some days are like that!' Ron Clear's brilliant airmanship saved G-ALFR when tests to evaluate extreme forward CG limits produced severe handling problems during landing. Damage was surprisingly light and the aircraft flew again within three weeks.

The other bits! A well-used photograph which inevitably carries the unbeatable caption 'Finished with engines.'

A delightful study of Ambassador and Consul at Christchurch.

Too good a picture to leave out! At the 1950 Farnborough Air Show, the Ambassador makes a stately approach over some of its airliner rivals.

Ambassador designer Arthur Hagg (right) talks to General Doolittle during his visit to discuss potential sales of the airliner to America.

Hagg, again in consultation, this time with ex-wartime Pathfinder Force leader, Don Bennett.

Three

Compton Abbas
Airfield

Located some three miles south of Shaftesbury and surrounded by rolling hills and deep valleys, Compton Abbas can lay a strong claim to being the most beautifully sited airfield in the British Isles. Opened in 1962 and owned since 1987 by Abbas Air, it lies some 800ft above sea level and boasts a 2,400ft-long landing area. Despite its almost total dedication to light aircraft and private flying, Compton Abbas did, on one noted occasion, experience the touch-down and departure of a much larger bird – a Hercules transport!

Yearly aircraft movements which now approach 35,000 consist mainly of training and pleasure flights, popular fly-ins and practice sessions for several locally-based aerobatic competition pilots. The airfield's managing director, Clive Hughes, has stated that he is intending to add to the natural attractions of Compton Abbas by staging a Dorset air show in the August 2000.

This pleasing study shows a Fairey Tipsy B of the Wagtail Flying Group at Compton Abbas in September 1971.

Another visitor in the early 1970s was this Thruxton Jackaroo.

Somewhat unusually carrying its registration letters across the fin and rudder is this Auster J/1 Alpha.

Informality is the order of the day at Compton Abbas as reflected in this aerial view taken in 1994.

A flight line to gladden the enthusiast's heart.

The colourful Stearman tends to dominate this miscellaneous group photographed in front of the airfield's restaurant.

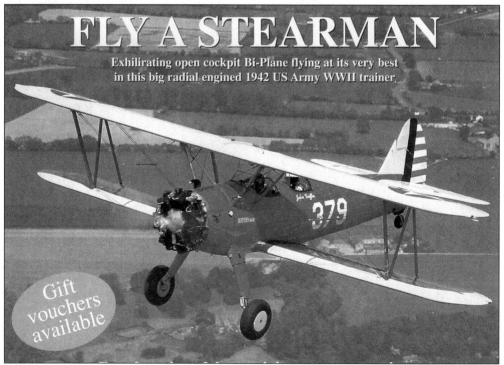

FLY A STEARMAN

Exhilirating open cockpit Bi-Plane flying at its very best in this big radial engined 1942 US Army WWII trainer

Gift vouchers available

Talking of Stearmans, John Griffin's PT-17 was built in 1942 by Boeing as the Kaydett basic trainer for the US Army Air Corps. Now resident at Compton Abbas, this popular machine provides joy-rides for the general public.

Another resident is this Slingsby Firefly owned and flown by aerobatic instructor Jez Hopkinson.

This study shows to perfection, man, mount and countryside. Paul Bonham flies the highly agile Sukhoi 31.

Up and over! A Yak 18T cavorts for the camera over Dorset's fields.

'The plane is front is a Toyota.' These Pitt Specials appear impatient to get into the air at a Compton Abbas aerobatic competition in 1994.

Dorset's green and pleasant land forms a perfect backdrop for a summer flying event.

Four

Poole Harbour –
RAF Hamworthy –
RNAS Sandbanks

For some nine years, from 1939 to 1948, the waters around Poole provided the bases for civil and military flying boats and seaplanes. Poole Harbour itself assumed a major significance when BOAC, officially formed on 1 April 1940, decided to transfer all flying boat operations, excluding maintenance, from its Hythe terminal at Southampton to supposedly safer confines further down the South Coast. Accordingly, Short 'C' and 'G' Class Empire flying boats, Catalinas and Sunderlands flew throughout the war from Poole via Foynes in Ireland and Botwood in Newfoundland to keep the airways open to and from the USA and along other routes to Africa, the Middle East and the Far East. As the transatlantic air links developed and the need for the US to abide by the Neutrality Act fell away following its entry into the war, BOAC set up a regular shuttle service to Ireland which allowed passengers from incoming Pan-American Clippers to be met. BOAC passengers on outgoing flights were accommodated at the nearby Harbour Heights hotel and were transferred to the waiting aircraft in motor launches which had all-women crews from the marine terminal at Poole Harbour Yacht Club's Saltern's Pier. This building also housed medical, immigration and customs facilities as well as certain airline and Ministry of Civil Aviation administrative functions. Incoming passengers were transported by the same hard-working ladies to Poole's quayside and received in what is today Poole Pottery's showrooms.

Twelve high-speed launches, built by the British Power Boat Company, also based in Poole from the start of the war, were operated by the corporation's Marine Department. In addition, the Ministry of Civil Aviation ran a fleet of fourteen launches for water control.

As a means of gaining optimum range and payload, Imperial Airways (forerunner of BOAC) had experimented with the unique Short-Mayo composite aircraft. It was the lower half of this 'piggyback' arrangement, the S.21 type flying boat 'Maia' that became the only Poole-based machine to be destroyed by enemy air attack. On the moonlit night of 3 May 1941, a lone Heinkel 111, seeing a 'target of opportunity', released a bomb which exploded nearby and caused the aircraft to sink. Rescuers were unable to save the night-watchman aboard and sadly he was drowned.

In early 1941, in order to replace lost aircraft, three Boeing 314As were purchased which, apart from conveying many notable wartime leaders to Stateside conferences, were soon employed on the West African route. At the end of the war, BOAC was instrumental in bringing home thousands of released prisoners from the Far East, the first arriving in Poole on 18 September 1945. By the end of that year, some twenty-four flying boats based at Poole were ready to embark on a passenger-carrying service which would log about 5,000,000 miles a year as civil air routes developed.

Poole's days were numbered, however. Commercial and land transportation considerations led to BOAC's return to Hythe in April 1948. The last two Solent class flying boats remained behind when an entrepreneur expressed an intention to join both hulls together to form a floating coffee bar but the project fell through. Today the only reminder of Poole's historic flying boat connection is an out-of-the-way sculpted stone commemorative panel set high in the wall of the town's municipal building.

As a result of the heavy bombardment sustained by the Royal Navy Seaplane School at Calshot on Southampton Water, in June 1940 the training of Fleet Air Arm pilots was transferred to what became RNAS Sandbanks, No.765 Squadron's mixed bag of Walrus, Swordfish, Kingfisher and Seafox floatplanes providing a marked contrast to the larger, more stately flying boats operated by BOAC and the RAF. Considered to be 'tiddlers' by the locals, the unit was quickly dubbed HMS Tadpole – a name which was formally adopted later by the Royal Navy when, after the seaplane training unit was disbanded in October 1943, the site became a pre-invasion landing-craft training establishment.

The RAF formed its own flying boat base at Poole in August 1942 when No.461 Squadron (Royal Australian Air Force) brought its complement of Short Sunderlands from Mountbatten, Plymouth. Although the new station was originally called RAF Poole, the name was changed to RAF Hamworthy almost immediately. The Sunderlands carried out anti-submarine patrols in the South-western Approaches and Bay of Biscay until No.210 Squadron's Catalinas took over those duties in May 1943. As with RNAS Sandbanks, RAF Hamworthy gave way to the landing craft training requirement in 1943, but flying boat activity resumed for a four-month spell in 1944 when Transport Command Sunderlands operated by BOAC crews flew personnel to the Middle East, India and Burma.

Today, Poole Pottery attracts thousands of customers from all over the world. In the war years, it provided passenger reception, security, customs and rest facilities for incoming travellers.

Poole Harbour Yacht Club looking resplendent in the summer sunshine in a picture taken in 1996. During the Second World War the building was requisitioned for use as the Marine Terminal for flying boat passengers.

Poole harbour pictured in peacetime with Brownsea Island in the background. The water channel shown here was designated 'No.3 Trot' (landing/mooring area) for BOAC's flying boats.

This panoramic view shows the Poole Harbour Yacht Club complex (lower centre) and Sandbanks (top centre). Swanage and Old Harry Rocks lie in the far distance.

'Maia' was sunk at its moorings in Poole harbour during a bombing attack on 3 May 1941.

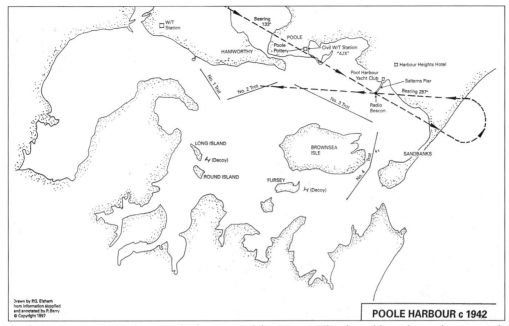

Poole Harbour, *c*.1942 showing the location of the 'Trots'. The dotted line shows the approach bearings used during landing.

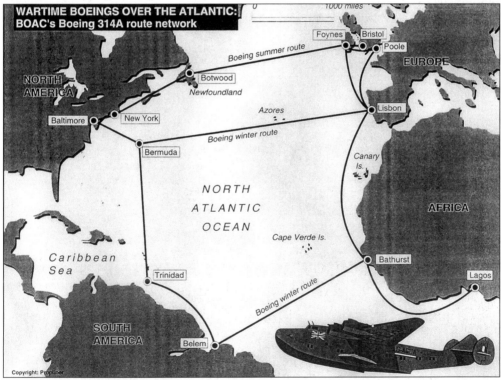

BOAC's Boeing 314As 'Bristol', 'Berwick' and 'Bangor' were soon put to work on the West African route. After each trip between Britain and Africa, the aircraft were flown to Baltimore for servicing.

On the step! 'Bristol' projects power and grace as it leaves the water. This aircraft took Winston Churchill to meet President Roosevelt in America departing from Stranraer on 17 June 1942 and returning nine days later.

'Bangor' sporting 'drab overall' camouflage disgorges passengers at Poole.

The launch depicts British Airways markings but, by the time this transport Sunderland joined the civil operation in March 1945, British Airways and Imperial Airways had long been merged to form BOAC.

'BOAC takes good care of you!' Supplies go aboard a motor launch moored along Poole's quayside.

Twenty-four Mk3 Sunderlands were converted to 'Hythe' class. This picture shows 'Hungerford' having undergone further conversion to become the sole Sandringham Mk1. Note the extra windows.

BOAC Speedbird 'Portsmouth', a Sandringham Mk5, was one of the Plymouth-class boats which operated on the post-war Poole-Sidney service.

Sandringham-by-the-Sea. A sight no longer seen after 1948 when BOAC withdrew its flying boat operations to Southampton.

A pride of Sandringhams await the breaker's axe at Hamworthy in the early 1950s.

Swansong for the Solents. 'City of Liverpool' and 'Solway' suffered an inglorious end, rotting away on Hamworthy beach after a suggested floating coffee bar project came to nothing.

The Walrus in its natural element. More often called the 'Shagbat', this amphibian formed part of No.765 Squadron at RNAS Sandbanks.

The Fairey Seafox was a lesser-known type that operated from Sandbanks.

More readily recognized in its land configuration, the Swordfish floatplane variant equipped No.700 W Squadron at Sandbanks before it embarked on HMS Fencer in September 1943.

Kingfishers seen over Poole Park!

A Vought-Sikorsky Kingfisher of No.765 Squadron leaving Sandbanks.

This rather war-weary Sunderland served with No.461 Squadron at Hamworthy.

No.210 Squadron Catalinas took over Coastal Command's convoy patrol duties following the Sunderland's departure for Pembroke Dock in April 1943.

Five

Royal Naval Air Station – HMS Osprey

Until the formal closure of the site and the amalgamation of its duties with RNAS Yeovilton on 31 March 1999, Portland could rightly claim to have encouraged the forceful slogan 'Fly Navy!' When, according to his log book, on 3 May 1912, Lieutenant (Acting Commander) Charles Rumney Samson RN undertook three flights in a Short S.38 floatplane from HMS *Hibernia*, he became the first man ever to fly from a moving ship. This event, which took place during the Portland Naval Review, is generally regarded as the birth of naval aviation. Within a few short years, the U-boats' deadly threat to British shipping in the First World War, led to the Admiralty positioning a chain of seaplane bases that included Portland (HMS *Serepta*) around the coast. It was from HMS *Serepta* that, on 28 September 1916, a flight of four Short floatplanes was formed to carry out anti-submarine patrols. However, when the Royal Air Force was formed on 1 April 1918, the Navy's aviation facilities were transferred to the new Service and the task was then undertaken by No.241 Squadron but this specialist role requirement was short-lived and the newly formed squadron was disbanded in 1919.

Twenty years later, as war loomed again, No.772 Squadron, equipped with Fairy Swordfish floatplanes and serving as a Fleet Requirements Unit, took up residence at Portland. Heavy German air attacks in 1940 precipitated a move to Ayrshire and it was not until 1946 that Sikorsky R-4B helicopters appeared, thus pioneering the use of rotary-wing aircraft within the Fleet.

On 14 April 1959, twelve Whirlwind helicopters of No.815 Squadron arrived from Eglington and formed the first unit of what officially developed into RNAS Portland (HMS *Osprey*). In August the same year, it was disbanded and re-formed as No.737 Squadron which became the Anti-Submarine Operational Flying School.

Throughout the sixties, Nos 771 and 829 Squadrons were responsible for various service trials and aircrew training along with Search and Rescue (SAR) duties. At this time, the air station expanded in a development scheme that reclaimed some twelve acres of land from Portland harbour.

After the new works programme was completed in 1973, the RN Pilotless Target Group (later renamed Fleet Target Group) moved across from the Dockyard area and No.772 Squadron took over the local SAR commitment. By 1982, two squadrons, Nos 815 and 702, were operating from Portland and, ten years later, No.829 joined with No.815 to form the largest helicopter squadron in Europe. During the 1990s, the Ministry of Defence introduced a new policy whereby certain traditional service functions were moved to the private sector and in 1995 the SAR obligation to the Dorset coast area was taken over by Bristow Helicopters. Wide-ranging defence cost studies also targeted Portland for closure and a run-down of activities began in 1998 with the Fleet Target Group transferring to RNAS Culdrose.

From small beginnings, when Portland-based seaplanes helped to keep the shipping routes open, Portland's air station moved on to mastermind the introduction of rotary-wing aircraft into Royal Navy operations. Now, its duty done, the station is no more, the site, alongside historic Portland Castle, being marked down for redevelopment.

On 3 May 1912 Lieutenant Samson took his place in history as the first man to fly off a moving ship, HMS *Hibernia*, during the Portland Naval Review. This feat was repeated on 9 May by Lieutenant Gregory.

The Short S.310 was used for patrol flights from RNAS stations around Britain's coast during the First World War.

Taken *c.*1900, this is one of the earliest photographs in existence showing the site of RNAS Portland.

The air station in 1969. The main administration building is in the centre.

The Westland Dragonfly served at Portland with No.771 Squadron from 1961 to 1963. VX 595 is displayed at the final Open Day on 17 October 1998.

Westland Whirlwind HAR 22s – licensed versions of the Sikorsky S 55 – also formed part of No.771 Squadron.

Whirlwind Mk3s and Mk7s flew with No.737 Squadron. XG 586, a hybrid Mk3/Mk7, is shown here in 1960.

The Westland Sea King entered service in August 1969. Shown here is the HC 4 variant, ZF 124 at Portland in March 1995.

A Whirlwind Mk7 practices rescue procedures off the Dorset coast.

A Westland Wessex, XM 838 of No.737 Squadron, offers a helping hand during a practice rescue operation.

A Wessex over Portland Castle.

The Westland Wasp helicopter fleet at Portland gave many years' faithful service before the type was retired in March 1988.

The reclaimed land was used to provide the heliport area (centre).

The final view of RNAS Portland, taken late in 1997.

Top left: A rather colourful view of the Air Station taken in 1977 showing HAS 3 and HAR-5 Wessex and HAS 1 Wasp helicopters.

Left: Looking eastwards over the Air Station in 1986. In the background the new Wardroom and Senior Rates' Mess are under construction.

A No.815 Squadron Lynx over Portland Bill marks the end of an era for Dorset's naval helicopter crews.

Six

Tarrant Rushton

Returned to its former farmland status since closure in 1980, Tarrant Rushton, like so many contemporary wartime airfields, lies silent and virtually forgotten today. However, for an eventful period spanning nearly forty years, it was home to some three thousand servicemen and women as well as (from 1948) Sir Alan Cobham's Flight Refuelling Ltd.

Named after the nearby river Tarrant and village of Rushton, the airfield was built on requisitioned land in just seven months at a cost of £1m. The initial hand-over to the RAF took place on 17 May 1943 but, as an event on the wartime calendar, it was somewhat overshadowed by the famous raid carried out by the Dambusters the night before. The formal opening of the station in October 1943 was quickly followed by the formation of 298 and 644 Squadrons and both units, flying Halifax aircraft, remained in residence until mid-1945. No.196 Squadron, equipped with Stirlings, also took part in what became a major airborne operations-training programme at Tarrant Rushton in the months leading up to D-Day.

Many famous service leaders including Eisenhower, Montgomery, Trafford Leigh-Mallory and (though by then long retired) Lord Trenchard visited the Dorset base to witness massed paratroop drops and day and night take-offs which tested to the full the skills of the RAF and Glider Pilot Regiment crews. In addition to all this highly visible activity, other more covert operations were taking place. In April 1944, Halifaxes flew from Tarrant Rushton carrying supplies for the French Resistance, and Special Operations Executive agents, including the legendary 'Odette', were parachuted into occupied Europe. Several squadrons normally based elsewhere frequently used Tarrant Rushton as a forward take-off point for raids on mainland Europe.

The first airborne unit to land in Normandy on 6 June 1944 was the 1st Platoon of 'D' Company, 2nd Battalion Oxford & Buckinghamshire Light Infantry, led by Major John Howard. This advance force, consisting of one hundred and seventy-one men left Tarrant Rushton's mile-long runway at forty-second intervals in six Horsa gliders to attack and capture bridges over the Caen Canal and Orne River. The brilliance of their successful achievement proved inspirational and a fine reflection on the extensive training that preceded the raid. In addition to D-Day, Tarrant Rushton's squadrons also took part in Operation Market Garden, the ill-fated attack on Arnhem, and Operation Varsity, the crossing of the Rhine. During the summer of 1944, Tarrant Rushton's aircraft dropped heavily-armed crack units of the Special Air Service, complete with Jeep transports behind enemy lines. The aim was to disrupt German communications and to assist the allied forces' progress towards Berlin. Missions to support Resistance groups continued throughout 1944 with ten-hour flights to Norway and Denmark proving the most demanding in terms of fuel management and navigational skill.

When peace came, 298 Squadron moved out to India and 644 to Palestine which left 295 and 297 as the final residents until the station closed in September 1946. Throughout the war years, RAF Tarrant Rushton was commanded by Group Captain T.B. Cooper OBE DFC, an officer who, always held in high regard, was sadly to lose his life while flying a Meteor from Boscombe Down on 6 March 1949.

In 1948, the ex-wartime base became home to Sir Alan Cobham's Flight Refuelling Ltd. At this time, the company was developing aerial refuelling systems and it was as a result of interest shown by the US Air Force that the 'probe and drogue' system, now in world-wide use, originated. Flight Refuelling also became heavily involved in the Berlin Airlift with its fleet of thirteen Lancaster and Lancastrian tankers based in West Germany returning regularly to Tarrant Rushton for maintenance work. Throughout its thirty-year tenure, the company was engaged in major repair, modification and overhaul programmes for aircraft belonging to the Royal Air Force and other countries. One major contract involved the conversion of well over two hundred Meteors to the pilotless drone configuration. Another major undertaking by Flight Refuelling was the administration and operation of the RAF's No.210 Advanced Flying School. Formed on 5 August 1952 and disbanded on 13 March 1954, it operated Meteor F.3, Meteor T.7 and Vampire FB.5 aircraft. As the company expanded, a new factory was built at nearby Wimborne to accommodate its manufacturing activities, but flight-testing concerned with air-to-air refuelling and target systems development continued at Tarrant Rushton until 1980.

The airfield's chequered history is today recorded on a memorial plaque that was unveiled on 6 June 1982, exactly thirty-seven years after the momentous departure of men and machines from the station on D-Day.

Tarrant Rushton's control tower, pictured in 1979, just a year before the airfield's closure. The glasshouse on the roof was added by Flight Refuelling Ltd in the early 1950s.

RAF Tarrant Rushton, 1943. The runway running straight ahead is the mile-long 01/19 with 08/26 running left to right and 13/31 running diagonally from top left to bottom right.

Weapons and supplies were dropped to French Resistance teams from Halifaxes based at Tarrant Rushton.

Training for D-Day 1944. An Airspeed Horsa already painted with its 'invasion stripes' comes in fast and low to land in the grass triangle between the runways.

Stirling nil, Halifax nil! The score-line shows no-one emerging a winner after this unfortunate entanglement at Tarrant Rushton in March 1944. Surprisingly, there were no human casualties.

The Finger Inn was a popular part of the officers' mess at Tarrant Rushton. Centre stage is Captain Bernard Halsall of the Glider Pilot Regiment.

A seven-tonne Tetrach tank makes its way out of a Hamilcar glider with minimum clearance at Tarrant Rushton early in 1944.

A Halifax tug and Horsa glider combination blend into the Dorset countryside.

A Halifax tug and Hamilcar glider fly over the Blandford army camp during the work-up period prior to D-Day.

Perhaps the most dramatic picture taken of a towed take-off. A Halifax claws into the air with its captive Horsa from Tarrant Rushton.

Cometh the hour! Taken at 6.00 p.m. on Tuesday 6 June 1944, this well-used photograph was taken from the station's Tiger Moth, just before the airfield's third lift on D-Day. About to take part in Operation Mallard were Horsa and Hamilcar gliders along with Halifax tugs of Nos 298 and 644 Squadrons.

One of Tarrant Rushton's characters was Buster Briggs – shown here with a Hurricane that he spotted abandoned in France while flying a glider retrieval flight after D-Day. On his return, he persuaded his squadron engine and airframe fitters to go to Normandy to inspect and repair the aircraft, and then flew it back to Tarrant Rushton.

More gliders – this time Operation Market Garden – and the scene at Tarrant Rushton before the ill-fated attempt to capture the bridge at Arnhem in September 1944.

One day after the airborne landing at Arnhem. This reconnaissance photograph shows fierce fighting taking place only a hundred yards north of the bridge.

Casualties from the Arnhem operation are offloaded from a Dakota transport at Tarrant Rushton.

An impressive scene as Tarrant Rushton's No.298 Squadron (left) and No.644 Squadron (right) prepare to tow an airborne army of Hamilcar gliders from Woodbridge (near Ipswich) for the crossing of the Rhine in March 1945.

The only known picture of RAF Tarrant Rushton's wartime station commander, Group Captain TB Cooper (right). He is seen here welcoming Air Vice Marshal Scarlett-Streatfield who had arrived to present No.644 Squadron with a new crest in April 1945.

AVM Scarlett-Streatfield presents the new crest to No.644 Squadron's commanding officer, Wing Commander Leonard Archer. Tragically the AVM was to die in a flight to Norway less than a month later.

Tea break at Tarrant Rushton. Flight Refuelling's staff worked around the clock to maintain its Lancastrian/Lancaster fleet engaged on the Berlin Airlift 1948-1949.

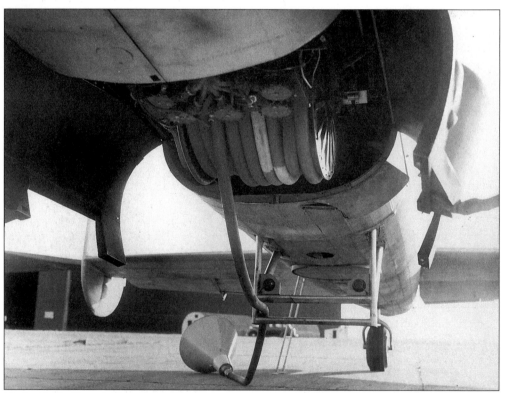

Flight Refuelling Ltd undertook air-to-air refuelling trials using converted Lancasters in the post-war period. Shown here is tanker equipment used for early 'probe and drogue' trials in 1949.

Flight Refuelling's Pat Hornidge flew a Meteor Mk III for twelve hours to secure an endurance record for jet aircraft in August 1949. His aircraft was refuelled ten times by the company's Lancaster flown by Tom Marks.

The 'business end' of Hornidge's record-breaking Meteor.

The United States Air Force sent four B-29s and two F-84s to Tarrant Rushton in 1950 for the installation of 'probe and drogue' refuelling equipment.

Two F-84s equipped with wing-mounted probes carried out the first in-flight-refuelled crossing of the Atlantic by jet aircraft in September 1950.

Bristol Brigands were converted from the B.2 bomber to T.4 training standard by Flight Refuelling in the early 1950s.

Some 650 Meteors of various Marks underwent repair and modification in Flight Refuelling's Tarrant Rushton hangars. In addition, the company administered the RAF's No.210 Advanced Flying School throughout 1953 when this picture was taken.

Over two hundred Meteors were also converted to the unmanned drone configuration at Tarrant Rushton in the 1950s.

Tarrant Rushton was one of several sites designated as a diversionary airfield for the RAF's 'V' Bomber Force. Valiants are shown here during a Quick Reaction Alert exercise in the early 1960s.

During the 1960s, Flight Refuelling designed and developed the Rushton Target Winch. Targets could be deployed up to some eight miles behind the towing aircraft.

A U Mk16 drone aircraft being cleared for a (manned) test flight.

Carried on Canberra WJ632, the Rushton winch and target system was first flown on 29 September 1966.

A frequent visitor to Tarrant Rushton in the 1960s was this Belgian Air Force Fairchild C-119 C. Flight Refuelling Ltd was at this time carrying out a major repair and modification programme on BAF F-84s and T-33s.

Canberra WV 787 carried out highly secret tests that included the spraying of microbiological spores over Tarrant Rushton in April 1967. The spray boom is shown stowed under the rear fuselage.

The Hawker P.1127, XP 980 had its profile increased to represent a two-seat Harrier when it carried out barrier-net trials at Tarrant Rushton in 1971.

In June 1982, hundreds of veterans and their families, along with Flight Refuelling's ex-airfield personnel, gathered to witness the unveiling of a memorial stone at Tarrant Rushton's main entrance. The event included a fly-past by Battle of Britain Flight's Lancaster PA 474 which had at one time been sent to this very spot for conversion to a drone target!

This plaque commemorates the units, both military and civil, which operated from Tarrant Rushton.

Today all is quiet and peaceful and midst the waving corn, poppies hang their heads seemingly in silent tribute to the many who lost their lives having flown from Tarrant Rushton.

Seven

RAF Warmwell
(Woodsford)

Constructed as part of the government's pre-war Royal Air Force expansion scheme, 6 Armament Training Camp (ATC), RAF Woodsford situated some four miles east of Dorcheser, provided aircrew gunnery and bombing instruction. Although work on the site was not completed by the time the station was formally opened on 1 May 1937, when training began, the unit's aircraft were accommodated at a satellite airfield at nearby Chickerell. The location of practice ranges on Chesil Beach aroused strong feelings locally. Environmental and wild life conservation groups protested strongly, citing the detrimental effect low-flying aircraft and gunfire would have on the inhabitants of the nearby Abbotsbury Swannery, but it was all to no avail. In the event, the bird population easily absorbed the disturbances caused by the new aerial intruders and life continued much as before. As a consequence of possible confusion between the similarly- named Woodsford and Woodford, the Avro factory airfield near Manchester, on 1 July 1938, the Station became known as Warmwell.

Using Westland Wallace biplanes as its primary target-towing aircraft, the Station provided varied armament training for Hawker Hind, Bristol Blenheim and Fairey Battle crews from many regular and auxiliary squadrons. The formation of 10 Air Observers' School (AOS), soon renamed 10 Bombing and Gunnery School (B and GS) also coincided with a further expansion of the airfield and its elevation to 'forward operational airfield' status within Fighter Command's 10 Group in 1939.

As the Battle of Britain gathered pace, Warmwell's location within a few minutes' flying time of the south coast proved of crucial importance. 609 Squadron equipped with Hurricanes moved to Warmwell, primarily to assist in the defence of Portland's harbour and naval establishment – the most heavily attacked target after London and Liverpool. 152 Squadron's Spitfires also shared the Station and in addition to often having to defend their own base against enemy attack, both squadrons were in constant action as the Luftwaffe's massed formations headed inland towards Yeovil and Bristol.

From 1941, a succession of Fighter Command squadrons based at Warmwell regularly carried out offensive strikes on German shipping and land-based targets. 175 Squadron, having temporarily moved forward to RAF Ford in Sussex, took part in Operation Jubilee, the infamous combined attack on Dieppe on 19 August 1942, its Hurricane fighter-bombers striking gun emplacements on the coast. The following month, Westland Whirlwind fighter-bombers of 263 Squadron along with Hawker Typhoons belonging to 266 Squadron arrived at Warmwell to continue the routine of armed reconnaissance flights and coastal convoy patrols interspersed with harassing attacks on mainland military installations.

Although the US 8th Air Force's 307th Fighter Squadron attended Warmwell's Armament Practice Camp for a brief spell in July 1942, it was the arrival of the 474th Fighter Group and the redesignation of 'RAF Warmwell' to 'Station 454 USAAF' in March 1944 that confirmed the fact that the Yanks were definitely over here. The Group's Lockheed P-38J Lightnings were also converted to the fighter-bomber role and began operational flying in late April, attacking German coastal defences as part of the aerial 'softening up' process prior to the D-Day invasion. However, by August, the Americans had moved on to the continent and with the skies over Dorset now much calmer, command of the Station was returned to the RAF.

Warmwell's 'hour of glory' had been and gone and although Armament Practice Camp training continued for another year or so, the Station was placed under a Care and Maintenance order in October 1945. It is not surprising that Warmwell's fighting personnel experienced tragedy in both handing out and receiving the blows of war. Many who lost their lives whilst flying from the Station have no known graves, as numerous battles were fought out over the sea, but of the twenty-six names (including those who died on the ground during enemy attack) that grace the Station's Roll of Honour, most rest peacefully together under Dorset soil in Warmwell's beautifully evocative churchyard.

The ensuing years have seen the old airfield site, once home to over eight hundred personnel, ravaged by extensive sand and gravel quarrying and the encroachment of local housing estates. However one or two physical reminders of those far-off days do remain. Two Bellman hangars and some dispersal hardstandings are used for agricultural purposes, and though now heavily overgrown, a few brick buildings and fighter pens can easily be found in nearby Knighton Woods. Prior to its conversion to a private dwelling, Egdon House, now sited alongside a road that follows the airfield's original northern perimeter track, was once the Station Watch Tower; but perhaps the most poignant and fitting tribute to Warmwell's illustrious past lies in the Purbeck stone memorial that was formally dedicated on the old communal site on 11 June 1989 in the presence of many veterans.

Although antiquated by 1937, this Westland Wallace II served as a drogue target tower with No.6 Armament Training Camp.

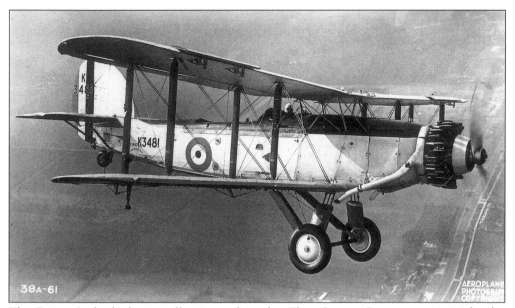

The Fairey Seal which normally operated in the 'Fleet Spotter Reconnaissance' role also equipped No.6 ATC.

Among visitors to Warmwell in 1938 were the Hawker Hind light bombers from XV Squadron at Abingdon. (Note the unique Roman numeral squadron identification on the fuselage.)

Boulton & Paul Overstrands, along with Fairey Seals, Hawker Hinds and Handley Page Harrows were the main workhorses of No.10 Air Observers' School.

The Handley Page Harrow provided modern equipment for No.10 AOS.

The Empire Air Day held at Warmwell in 1938 saw a visit by a Handley Page Heyford bomber.

Pre-sortie preparations on this No.257 Squadron Typhoon include engine inspection, arming and refuelling.

'Come on lads, you can do it.' Armourers load a 250lb bomb onto a Whirlwind fighter-bomber in Warmwell's Knighton Woods.

A peaceful setting belies this Whirlwind's warlike intentions.

Warmwell's Holy Trinity churchyard is the final resting place for twenty-two airmen.